DRINKING WITH DEAD WOMEN WRITERS

ELAINE AMBROSE
AK TURNER

Mill Park Publishing
Eagle, Idaho
www.MillParkPublishing.com

Text copyright © 2012 by **Elaine Ambrose** and **AK Turner**

Front cover artwork by **Ward Hooper**

Design and layout by **Blake Beckman, iRockimages.com**

Back cover photograph by **LeAna Earley**

This is a work of historical fiction. Stories of drinking with Ambrose and Turner, while entertaining and clever, are fiction.

ISBN 978-0-9728225

Printed in the USA

Mill Park Publishing
Eagle, ID 83616
www.MillParkPublishing.com

"Drink and dance and laugh and lie,
love the reeling midnight through,
for tomorrow we shall die
(but alas we never do)!"

–Dorothy Parker

CONTENTS

Introduction 7

Margaret Mead
Scientific Anthropology Vs. Smut 9

Willa Cather
Ghosts Knocking 13

Jane Austen
A Sensible Prejudice for Spruce Beer 17

Sylvia Plath
If I Knew You Were Coming 21

Erma Bombeck
Laughing Until Tequila Runs out Our Noses 25

The Brontë Sisters
The Rum Trail 31

Emily Dickinson
Dwelling in Possibility and Paranoia 35

Carson McCullers
Queen Bee 41

Margaret Mitchell
Civility and Civil War 45

Dorothy Parker
Fug 51

George Eliot
Ugly Girls Write Better Than Men 55

Virginia Woolf
Drink Only Wine 59

Edna St. Vincent Millay
Burning the Candle at Both Ends 63

Flannery O'Connor
Birds of a Feather 69

Louisa May Alcott
Little Women, Big Whiskey 73

Ayn Rand
The Philosophy of Vodka 77

Selected Works of Dead Women Writers 81

INTRODUCTION

Blame it on the Cabernet. We met to share libations and laughter, but in less than an hour had outlined a book. We'd capitalize on our proven talents for drinking and our evolving talents for writing, while incorporating literary flair by including 16 famous female authors. Game on.

We agreed to write and exchange chapters for eight weeks and publish the book within four months. Such goals are easy to set after swilling a few bottles of wine.

We met weekly to review progress, edit each other's stories, and, of course, consume a bottle of wine at The Grape Escape in Boise. Our imaginary interviews took us from Paris, France to lonely cemeteries, from the Russian Vodka Room in New York to the Silver Spur Saloon in Wendell, Idaho. We drank our way through two centuries of intriguing (but soberly dead) authors.

The best part of writing this book, besides sharing a case of wine, was the research. Many of the early authors used pen names because the general public didn't think women possessed literary talent. Hogwash! Several writers were recluses, some were suicides, and many had alternative sexual preferences. Their common characteristic was a passion to write. We invite readers to fill a glass, find a favorite chair, and join in our journey of drinking and chatting with dead women writers.

Elaine and AK

MARGARET MEAD
SCIENTIFIC ANTHROPOLOGY VS. SMUT

BY ELAINE AMBROSE

I met Margaret Mead sitting on a stone bench in the cemetery next to Trinity Episcopal Church in Buckingham, Pennsylvania. She stared at a modest tombstone perched in the grass. The inscription read: Margaret Mead, 1901 – 1978. "To Cherish the Life of the World."

She motioned for me to sit down and then opened a bottle of Bacardi Gold and poured it into two stoneware mugs decorated with Polynesian designs. We drank and allowed the smooth, dark rum to warm us against the cool breeze. She wore a loose dark suit and her brown hair was pulled back, revealing full cheeks and wise eyes.

"It's been over thirty years, but I still can't get used to the simple finality of this plain stone," she said. "In Samoa, the funeral ceremony includes grand feasts with whole cooked pigs and sweet puddings. The dead person is placed in the center of the room, and the village people bring gifts, money, and flowers. The elaborate event lasts for days. All I got was this meager headstone in the middle of a scraggly field."

"I've read your book, *Coming of Age in Samoa*," I said, sensing that a cemetery wasn't the most cheerful place to meet. "Your work established you as a respected, academic anthropologist. And your vast contributions to social science remain your lasting legacy, which is more important than this gravesite."

"Oh, I just needed an excuse to write about sex," she said. "Americans are still too uptight and could learn a lot from the natural practices of the Polynesian cultures. I still think the natives are more advanced than most of the people in modern society. They enjoy sex and don't need books, potions, or videos to explain how to do it."

I made a mental note to prune my erotica collection.

"You were an important speaker and writer during the sexual revolution of the 1960s," I said. "How did you cope with the harsh criticism of your work?"

Margaret snorted and washed down another drink.

"I wrote about what I observed," she said. "I lived in Samoa in a village of 600 people and studied 68 young women between the ages of 9 and 20. Their transition from childhood to adulthood didn't have any of the drama and emotional anxiety that American teens experience. Instead of making war, the natives made love. And that's what the peace movement in our country was trying to say. At first, my writings were rejected by academia and the general public, but attitudes now are becoming more lenient."

She refilled our mugs and took a long drink. I noted that the artwork etched into the mugs revealed naked natives enjoying various positions of copulation. I decided to search later for matching mugs to enhance my morning coffee.

"I taught at Columbia University during the 1970s," she said. "As liberated as those young women were, they still didn't have a clue about sex. I think every one of them should have studied in the South Pacific. If they did, you'd see a new generation of happier women."

"Your own life reveals your independent attitudes toward traditional relationships," I said.

"That's true. During my professional careers I lectured on the morals of anthropology while I was married three different times.

SCIENTIFIC ANTHROPOLOGY VS. SMUT

I also spent a lot of time with two female friends. The last 23 years with sweet Rhoda Metraux were full of true romance."

I decided to shift the conversation. "How have your experiences shaped your attitude toward child-rearing?"

"Well, I believe that children need the opportunity to learn that some people are loathsome and some are delightful," she answered. "I think that instead of needing lots of children, we need fewer, high-quality children. That remark always got me in hot water. But I only had one child, and she is proof of my assumption."

"I've read that you influenced the writings of renowned pediatrician Benjamin Spock."

"Yes, he was my daughter's doctor. He was totally wrong about breastfeeding. What do men know about breastfeeding? I told him that a mother should feed on the baby's demand and not have a set schedule. Can you imagine natives watching a clock before they fed their babies? That's ridiculous. Anyway, Dr. Spock eventually agreed with me and added that advice in his books."

"You also made a lasting impact on the feminist movement," I said.

"My book *Sex and Temperament in Three Primitive Societies* was celebrated by many women because it claimed that societies dominated by females have fewer problems. I studied several areas around Papua New Guinea in the Western Pacific. These communities embrace a pacifist culture that avoids warfare and violence. Wouldn't that be nice if our country could adopt those beliefs?"

"Life would certainly be easier," I replied. "I'd much rather drink rum and make love than go to war."

"I also believe that women should not be used in combat."

"Why?"

"Because they're too fierce!"

We laughed and took another drink.

"How do you think society can bring about cooperation among peoples?" I asked, feeling proud that my rum-doused brain could still verbalize a five-syllable word in a complete sentence.

11

"The answer can be simplified to bathrooms. Until the 1960s, our homes had one bathroom, and families worked out the logistics. Modern homes with two or more bathrooms have ruined the capacity to cooperate. If we aren't compelled to negotiate in the home, how do we learn to work within society?"

"Interesting analogy," I said, suddenly feeling guilty about my home's three bathrooms.

"But don't give up on our ability to change," she said. "Never doubt that a small group of thoughtful people could change the world. Indeed, it's the only thing that ever has."

"I understand why President Jimmy Carter posthumously awarded you the Presidential Medal of Freedom," I said. "The citation states that you mastered your discipline of cultural anthropology, and that you transcended it... intrepid, independent, plain spoken, and fearless."

"Yeah, and all I have is this puny grave marker," she said.

We laughed and finished our drinks. She took the mugs, wiped them with a printed cloth, and tucked them into her leather knapsack. Then she gently leaned the empty bottle against her headstone.

"It was so nice talking with you," she said as we walked away. "Always remember that you are absolutely unique. Just like everyone else."

WILLA CATHER
GHOSTS KNOCKING

BY AK TURNER

We're at Barrymore's on 13th Street, not far from her alma mater, the University of Nebraska. She tensed when I directed her down the alley, but in a former life the bar was a theater and the alley entrance used to be the performers' stage door. Inside, I'm instantly glad that I chose this place. The other bars overflowed with college kids and too much skin.

She has a kind, round face, punctuated with a nose drooping as if it wants to slide right off. I like her instantly, decide that she's kind. I want to put her at ease, because I worry that she's overwhelmed with what I know as the modern world, a world she left more than 65 years ago. I take her by the hand, which she doesn't resist, and lead her to a table. As we sit, she smoothes her skirts and a waitress approaches.

"What can I getcha?" she asks.

I look at Willa, still a bit frightened, and answer for us both. "Two Alaskan Ambers, please." The waitress disappears and Willa sits silent.

"So, what do you think?" I'm tentative.

"Well, I don't know," she sighs. "I worried that man would mistake living easily for living happily. But nothing of this," she looks around, left to right, then ceiling to floor, "looks easy. Everyone seems very complex."

"Yes and no," I say. "It may look complex, but most of us really are looking for the easy life as opposed to the happy one, just as you thought."

"It's... startling. This world seems to glow."

She's right, I realize. Everything has to do with light: neon, cell phones, flat screens.

"But I'd love to talk about you, in your life," I say. The waitress sets two pints of Amber on our table. Willa takes a timid taste, but then smiles at me, and again I feel the presence of kindness.

"My life," she says. "Well, I was born in '73 and died at age 73. I delivered mail on horseback when I was young. Everyone should experience work on land and with the land. It improves writing, especially the experiences of youth."

"But when you were young, you wanted to be a doctor, yes?"

"Yes, I did. Science is as intriguing as anything." We sit silent for a long moment and wade through the better part of our beers. It has never tasted so good.

"You wore men's clothing," I say, "and went by 'William.'"

I fear I've offended her, but she smiles. "Why not?"

I decide to change the subject because she seems so comfortable in her sensible skirt and jacket. "So, would your advice to an aspiring writer be to look to their youth?" I ask.

She looks up and to her right, thinking. At that moment, I wish she was my aunt and I her favorite niece. "Not necessarily," she says, bringing her eyes back and level with my own. "Whether writing or not, we'd all do well to remember the past, but not to dwell in it."

My beer is empty. I set it aside, retrieve a chewed ballpoint from my purse and attempt to write on my soggy napkin what she has just said. It's not working. The waitress brings another round.

"Let it go," Willa says, motioning to my failed scribble. "Remember, I'm the one who wanted my letters burned. Let's just enjoy the drink."

GHOSTS KNOCKING

We do just that, and we people-watch. Barrymore's seems filled with an unusually high number of extremely good-looking people. At first I think this is the bar as seen through beer goggles, but that's not the case. My eyes are true. The establishment just happens to attract hotties. But I only have a short time with Willa Cather, and hotties other than my husband have little effect on me, in any case, so I turn my attention back to the woman before me, the writer born 103 years before my own birth.

"Will you tell me a little bit more about writing?" I request.

"Yes, as long as you don't try to record it," she motions again to my napkin. "It's not a fear of my words being criticized, just that I can't bear to watch you struggle like that."

"Agreed," I grin.

She looks straight up, thinking again; I suppress the urge to pick up my pen.

"When it comes to writing," she looks me dead on, "your work is like a ghost knocking about in your head. It may haunt you continuously or lurk back in the shadows of your mind for decades, but that's what it is, a ghost. Your job, as the writer, is to find it a body, and that body is what will become the written words. It's not going to go away until you find it that body, because remember, it's not a memory or an idea, but a ghost that lives in your head until you find a way, a body, with which to free it."

My mind turns to hypnosis. Maybe I can hire a hypnotist later to take me back to this place so that I can remember and record everything she's saying. Because at this moment, there is no greater tragedy than that I cannot reflect upon these words later. It's almost devastating, the only saving grace is that I don't have much time left with her, so I must appreciate our remaining minutes.

We finish our second beers and I know that she doesn't have the energy for a third. She smiles politely. "I do have one question for you," she says.

"Of course."

"My wishes were respected, yes? My letters burned after I

15

died?"

"Yes," I say. I can't break her heart. I don't let her know what survived and what attempts have been made since her death to recount her whole being.

"There's something else," I say. "About Edith."

Her eyes light up at the mention of Edith. They lived together for almost 40 years.

"Yes?" she prompts.

"I just wanted you to know what Edith said of you after your death. I mean, about your death." I slow my speech, not from alcohol, but because I don't want to screw up my words. "She said that you were never more yourself than on the last morning of your life. She said that your spirit was high and your grasp of reality as firm as always."

She leans across the black shine of our table, puts her hand on mine and says, "Thank you."

Jane Austen
A Sensible Prejudice for Spruce Beer

BY ELAINE AMBROSE

Jane Austen and I walked into the Sherlock Holmes Pub in the Westminster area of London and found a table back in The Study. The crowds wouldn't come for another two hours, so we had the private room to ourselves. She ordered a plate of grilled goat cheese with balsamic vinegar, and I requested some crusty bread with olive oil and a pitcher of dark beer and two glasses. The beers arrived first, and we sipped the foam from the squatty pints.

"You just can't find good spruce beer anymore," Jane said, sighing as she licked her lips. "My father could make a fine batch of beer with just the right amount of needles and buds from our spruce trees near the Steventon Rectory."

"Wasn't your father a minister?" I asked.

"Yes, he was a rector of the Anglican Parish," she answered. "And he always drank beer, except on Sunday, of course."

The server brought the appetizers and turned away quickly, almost rude in his demeanor, but Jane wasn't annoyed.

"I do not want people to be agreeable, as it saves me the trouble of liking them," she said.

I nodded, remembering her famous quote, and we nibbled our food, washed it down with beer and poured another pint.

"Can you tell me about writing *Sense and Sensibility*?" I asked.

"You were only 35 years old."

She smiled and took another drink of beer.

"Well the original title was *Elinor and Marianne*. What a horrible title! It sounds like some kind of boutique in Liverpool."

"Was your family supportive of your writing?"

Jane set down her glass and momentarily stared out the window. I imagined her wandering back to her childhood home in Hampshire, England.

"Yes," she finally answered. "I had a large family, six brothers and one sister. I would read my stories to them. My father owned a large library and he encouraged my reading and writing. He gave me paper and fountain pens and bought me a writing table. Now people pay to see that little table in the museum. Sometimes I wander through and people approach and tell me I look like Jane Austen."

"You had a positive life at home?" I asked.

"I must have," she replied. "I never left. After my father died, my sister and I lived with our mother and we never married. I wrote books. She made beer. It was a great life."

"You write about relationships and you remained single," I said.

"Well, there was that innocent fling with Harris Bigg-Wither back in 1802. He had money and was hot with passion. I could get past his stutter and ugliness, but not his boorish behavior. At first I agreed to his marriage proposal, but then I changed my mind. As I've always said, happiness in marriage is entirely a matter of chance."

She finished her beer and we beckoned for another pitcher. A fresh and friendlier server arrived with a full pitcher and filled our pints. In the States, I prefer cold beer, but after consuming half a pitcher of stout pub beer served at room temperature, it tasted just fine.

"There was this dashing young lad who became Lord Chief Justice of Ireland," she continued. "Tommy Lefroy was his name but he changed that to Thomas after he became successful. I wrote to my sister Cassandra that I was almost afraid to tell her all the shocking and self-indulgent activities Tommy and I did together. But his family didn't like me and they sent him away. They were financially supporting him, and as I wrote in *Mansfield Park*, a large income is the best recipe for happiness. But, I imagine Tommy, or Thomas, often thought back on those youthful days of decadence with ample appreciation and a morsel of regret."

I silently enjoyed the fact that Jane Austen was a famous literary treasure and Tommy Lefroy and his judgmental family were all dead, gone, and forgotten. I also surmised that what was considered decadent in 1800 could be standard fare in today's programming for children.

"You wrote *Pride and Prejudice* just two years after *Sense and Sensibility*," I said. "Both novels are regarded as literary masterpieces; reviews in 1821 compared your work to Homer and Shakespeare, and they recently became big Hollywood movies, yet your name never appeared on the original manuscripts."

"That's how it was," Jane responded. "Women weren't regarded as having any literary talent, so the first books didn't name me as the author. But my father believed in me. In fact, he tried to pay Thomas Cadell, an established publisher in London, to publish an early version of *Pride and Prejudice* that I had titled *First Impressions*. The publisher rejected the offer."

"I appreciate the irony and parody in your writing," I said. "How were you drawn to focus on the games of love, particularly among the British upper classes?"

"Nothing amuses me more than the easy manner with which everybody settles the abundance of those who have a great deal less than themselves," she said. "I used that line in *Mansfield Park*. And in *Pride and Prejudice*, I wrote that vanity and pride are different things, though the words are often used synonymously. Pride relates more to our opinion of ourselves, vanity to what we would have others think of us."

"So, you write about the frailty of the human ego?" I asked.

"I write about life as I see it. As in this passage in *Emma:* Silly things do cease to be silly if they are done by sensible people in an impudent way."

"Are you surprised by your success now?"

Jane laughed. "I've heard that there are several chapters of the Jane Austen Society. And there are international essay contests, entire college curriculums based upon my work, and books written about my books. I ranked 70 in a list of '100 Greatest Britons,' and my books have been used as the basis for television shows and web sites. I do get a kick out of all the fuss."

Patrons began to fill the pub as we concluded our visit, and the noise and commotion caused Jane to cover her ears.

"I'd rather be sitting in the shade on a fine day," she said. "Looking upon the pastures is the most perfect refreshment."

We walked out of the pub and into the fog along Northumberland Street.

"Oh, one more thing," she said. "The history books say that I died of bovine tuberculosis, a disease associated with drinking unpasteurized milk. That's poppycock. I died because it was time to go. Come and see me sometime at Winchester Cathedral. I'll be hovering over the nave, making fun of pompous people."

SYLVIA PLATH
IF I KNEW YOU WERE COMING

BY AK TURNER

"**I** make you nervous," states Sylvia Plath.

She's right, of course, though there's no reason why this should be so. Sure, she's swallowed pills and ultimately stuck her head in the oven, but it's not like she can do anything now. Surely she won't produce a gun from her pocket and blow her brains out in front of me while we're sharing a pint. At least, I hope not.

"Oh, not at all," I lie. "I'm just great." I'm an atrocious liar.

"Well, you obviously know about me, so why don't you tell me about you," she says. "But please, whatever you do, don't tell me you're a writer. I don't think I could stand it."

I know that she's hoping for something entirely practical. My experiences fishing and farming were so brief that I don't think I could effectively bullshit my way through them. There is one thing I do know: scrubbing toilets.

"I'm a housecleaner," I say.

"Oh!" she looks delighted. "A maid?"

"Yes," I smile. "These days people call it housecleaner, but yes, same thing. I clean houses."

"Thank goodness. I was afraid you were going to babble about your yearning for successful artistic expression or something equally insufferable."

"We wouldn't want that," I affirm.

"Are you married?" she asks.

"Yes." It comes out almost as a hiss. When it ends I find I'm holding my breath.

She looks me dead on with a smile bordering on smirk. She's enjoying my squirm and draws it out further by ordering two more. We're at the Ship & Shovell in Charing Cross where a pint is truly a pint. My head is light, which makes me think again of her head in the oven.

"What is unsettling to you right now?" she asks. "Your own marriage? Or are you thinking of Ted?"

"My marriage isn't unsettling at all!" I insist. Then, tentatively, "Do you want to talk about Ted?"

"Why not?" she smiles. "Life wasn't depressing enough while I endured it. Let's dwell on Ted for a bit. After that maybe we can go in for some electroshock therapy together, what do you say?"

I'm speechless.

"I'm joking, of course! Don't worry. It's all over, so sure we can talk about Ted. What do you want to know?"

"What do you remember most?" I ask.

"Sometimes it's the misery of the latter part, but often it's the passion of the beginning. Being consumed with each other. Consuming one another. We were violent. Often out of anger, but equally often out of pure need. Either way, it was always poison. I imagine it was much the same with Assia."

Even in my fogged state of mind, I remember that Plath and Ted Hughes parted not long after she learned of his affair with Assia Wevill.

"It may have been," I say. "She killed herself, too."

"Really?"

"Yes, about six years after you died. She killed herself and their four-year-old daughter."

"They had a daughter and she took the child, too?"

I nod. Her face goes blank and we sip in silence for a moment.

IF I KNEW YOU WERE COMING

I need to change the subject. Before I can, she asks, "How did she do it?"

"Gas."

"At least I had the sense to protect my children," she says. This is debatable, but I feel like I may go stick my own head in the oven if we don't get to another topic soon.

"There's something else I want to tell you," I smile.

"What's that?" she looks suspicious.

"You won a Pulitzer."

"I did?" Her smile is almost as audible as her voice. Patrons of the Ship & Shovell raise their glasses to her in quiet congratulations.

"When?"

"1982."

"Huh," her brow furrows. "Sure took them long enough." I refrain from telling her that it was for *The Collected Poems* and that Hughes, her two-timing ex-lover, provided both an edit and an introduction. I don't know how she'd feel about it and am terrified to find out. I guess correctly at her next question. "Ted never won a Pulitzer, did he?"

"No," I say. I'm not about to tell her of the recognition he did receive, of which there was plenty.

"That's really all I need to know," she says. "That makes this," she gestures to the pub around us, holding us in with wood and alcohol, "worth a brief return."

"I'm glad," I say.

"Let's get back to you," she says. "Did you always want to be a maid? I mean, a home cleaning person?"

"Um, n-no," I stutter. "I actually wanted to be a doctor but found it too difficult a course of study." This is a lie. I've never wanted to be a doctor. The part about it being too difficult is undoubtedly true. Perhaps I should have come up with a desired occupation closer to my own truth, but I can't help but cater to the dead.

"Me, too!" she says. "The practicality of it, the usefulness! It's glorious even to think about – work that doesn't require the emotional devastation of art!"

I imagine that many aspects of medicine have equal parts of emotional devastation, but I'm finding that time spent with Sylvia Plath involves a lot of tongue-biting.

"But the cleaning," she continues, calm again, "you enjoy that, do you?"

"I do," I admit. This is half true. I enjoy cleaning the average home. I detest cleaning the homes of hoarders or the incredibly rich.

"You must get quite an insight into people's lives when you see all of their dirty details."

"Oh yes, absolutely."

"Do you look at what they hope to keep hidden?" she asks. Her voice has dropped to a whisper; we're now a schoolgirl confessional.

"Only when they're stupid enough to leave secrets in plain sight," I answer. She sits back, satisfied with this.

"What's the worst thing about cleaning houses?" she asks.

I answer honestly, because I've lied too much already. I give her the truth because it's really all that I have left to offer. "Fear of finding a suicide."

ERMA BOMBECK

LAUGHING UNTIL TEQUILA RUNS OUT OUR NOSES

BY ELAINE AMBROSE

"Hot damn," I exclaimed as I stepped out of the taxi at the Old Town Tortilla Factory in Scottsdale, Arizona. "It's time for Happy Hour in the gazebo!"

I knew the place would be fun when I saw a sign boasting 120 premium tequilas. An afternoon of Erma Bombeck and margaritas was all I needed to survive the oppressive Arizona heat. I joined Erma at the bar and grabbed some cloth napkins to blot my forehead. A charming bartender named Roberto brought me a tall glass of ice water after he noticed me sweating like a prize fighter.

"Allow me to recommend the Millionaire's Margarita, a lovely concoction of Jose Cuervo Reserva, 150-year Celebration Grand Marnier, and fresh squeezed lime juice," he said with a wink. "It's just what you need to be cool."

"Bring us a pitcher," Erma demanded. "I can't see wasting money by sucking down drinks at $19 each. And, heaven knows, we want to be cool."

Roberto returned with a cold pitcher of margaritas and two frosted glasses. I fought the urge to rub the glass over my face.

"I've always wanted to meet you," I said, "ever since you wrote that, in your family, gravy was considered a beverage."

"I just wrote about life and somehow people liked it," she said as she took a sip. "And these are the best margaritas in town. It was at this very table that I wrote the line, 'Never accept a drink from a urologist!'"

I nodded in agreement and then remarked about how her humorous newspaper columns had been cut out and taped to millions of refrigerators from 1965 to 1996. I asked how a suburban housewife from Ohio achieved the distinction of attracting 30 million readers to her columns in 900 newspapers and how she wrote 15 books, most of them bestsellers.

"Well, the answer is clear, my dear," she said slowly. "I'm funny."

Erma began writing newspaper columns on a portable electric typewriter on a wobbly desk in her bedroom. She parlayed her incredible humor and sassy attitude to regular appearances on radio and television. She made one million dollars a year by the late 1980s, but retained her unaffected demeanor.

Roberto noticed our pitcher was empty and magically appeared with another one. After convincing him that we were incognito restaurant reviewers, he hurried over with a complimentary quesadilla stuffed with pesto, tomatoes, vegetables, beans and sour cream. We needed the food to help sop up the tequila.

Erma noticed my bulging briefcase next to her sensible purse.

"I'm amazed at all the crap you women now carry around with you: cell phones with Internet access and laptop computers that check your spelling, edit your grammar, format your pages and play music while you write. What if your power goes out? Or what if your kid pukes on your keyboard? That happened to me several times but I just threw everything into the sink and sprayed it off."

"How did you do it all?" I asked. "You had children and you worked from home. How did you finish three weekly columns and find time for all your other responsibilities?"

"Oh, that was easy. I just locked myself in my bedroom," Erma said. "And you know what? Those kids grew up just as fine as could be. Today's parents worry way too much about tending to their kids. Have you ever heard of helicopter parents? They're the ones who follow their kids to college to help them blow their noses and wipe their butts. Those kids couldn't pass gas without their mother's interference, let alone pass a class. I take a very practical view of raising children. I put a sign in each of their rooms: Checkout Time is 18 years! I got over trying to be the perfect mother. Sure, there was some guilt. But, as I always say, guilt is the gift that keeps on giving."

"You became successful during an era when all the magazine advertisements portrayed thin women dressed in pearls and cooking gourmet dinners for their adoring husbands," I said, shuddering at the thought. "Yet, your comments about housework brought laughs from a generation of women."

"Well, I believe that no one ever died from sleeping in an unmade bed, and that if the item didn't multiply, smell, catch fire, or block the refrigerator door, let it be. No one else cared, so why should you?" she said. "And what idiot decided that Little League uniforms should be white?"

We shook our heads in mutual puzzlement. "Those uniforms should all be black," I said. "And disposable, like those silly garments we wear at the doctor's office."

"Did you know that my second favorite household chore is ironing? My first is hitting my head on the top bunk bed until I faint. Housework, if you do it right, will eventually kill you."

We clinked our glasses in agreement. I wondered if I should be taking notes because I didn't want to forget all these wonderful tidbits of knowledge. I decided to drink more margaritas instead.

"You set the bar for future women journalists," I said. "What advice do you have for the younger generation?"

"Drink lots of margaritas," she said. "But, seriously, I've always defended women in the workplace. I was involved in the Presidential Advisory Committee for Women and we worked to get the Equal Rights Amendment passed. I got a lot of criticism for my advocacy and some bookstores even removed my books! Can you imagine how stupid they were? I really was disappointed when the amendment didn't pass. We tried for seven years but we couldn't get those three states to ratify it. I love living in Arizona, but sometimes the conservative politics are really asinine."

We touched our glasses together and murmured support for our oppressed sisters. Roberto, who was getting cuter by the drink, brought us some chips and salsa. We dove into the basket like frenzied ferrets.

"I keep trying to go on a diet," Erma said as she snatched another chip. "And I tried going to the gym. I've exercised with women so thin that buzzards followed them to their cars. In two decades, I've lost a total of 789 pounds. I should be hanging from a charm bracelet."

"Don't make me laugh when I'm drinking or I'll shoot tequila out of my nose," I said. "Did you really have a weight problem?"

"No, I have an eating problem," she answered, "and I'm just about to fight you for those crumbs on the table."

We laughed out loud as we dueled for the remaining chips.

Erma came up for air. "And I'm sick of politics. I haven't trusted polls since I read that 62% of women had affairs during their lunch hour. I've never met a woman in my life who would give up lunch for sex! At least Bill was a wonderful husband," she continued. "But marriage has no guarantee. If that's what you're looking for, go live with a car battery. I also believe that God created man, but I could do better."

At that point, we dug out photos of our kids and husbands. Erma reminded me that her children refused to eat anything that hadn't danced on television. I replied that the rules hadn't changed all that much.

"Children make your life important," Erma said. "I always told mine not to confuse fame with success. Madonna is one; Helen Keller is the other."

Roberto, by now the cutest bartender in the whole world, reminded us that Happy Hour was over and so was his shift. We eagerly paid for our evening's refreshments and decided it was cool enough to venture back outside.

"Whatever you do, keep on writing," Erma said. "I even wrote my own epitaph. It said, 'I told you I was sick.'"

Roberto passed us in the parking lot and honked the horn on his new red Camaro. "Tips must be good," I said. "That guy must sell a ton of Millionaire's Margaritas."

"Good for him! I always told my children to never give up," she said as we walked toward waiting taxis. "I failed most of my literary assignments at Ohio University and was rejected for a job with the university newspaper." She paused for effect and then snorted, "I win."

DRINKING WITH DEAD WOMEN WRITERS

THE BRONTË SISTERS
THE RUM TRAIL

BY AK TURNER

It wasn't easy meeting up with the Brontë sisters. Emily wanted nothing but home, Charlotte kept pushing for Brussels, and Anne seemed to think there was a place in Africa called "Angria" that would be suitable. Severe miscommunication, combined with the impossibility of four women (three of them dead) trying to agree on a meeting spot, almost caused me to travel to Haworth, New Jersey, where I would have waited in vain for a very long time. Somehow we converge on something called The Rum Trail in Manchester. It starts at Keko Moku where the shirtless bartender is lighting booze on fire. Charlotte, Emily and Anne look so delicate and frightened that I fear they might die all over again.

"Let's keep our morals intact," whispers Charlotte to her sisters.

"Yes," agrees Anne, eyeing the bartender, "but did you see his chest?"

"I can't believe I'm drinking rum with the Brontë sisters!" I say.

"No," shushes Emily, "we'd prefer it if you called us the Bell brothers."

I note their skirts, the curls framing Anne's face. "You think someone is going to mistake you for brothers?" I ask.

"I miss Branwell," says Emily.

"Let's not talk of brother," says Anne, still drinking in the bartender's chest as well as his cocktail.

Before I know it we're buzzed and heading to the second stop on The Rum Trail. The Hula Tiki Lounge boasts hedonistic fun. I'd fear for Charlotte's high morals, but she's looking sufficiently looped. Emily's equally saturated, but embracing the next cocktail. "Have you been to Haworth? It's lovely." She teeters and I grab her arm to steady her.

Out of sight of the bartender from Keko Moku, Anne is eager to return to the topic of her brother. "Don't let them tell you Branwell died of tuberculosis. Yes, it was the bane of our family, but in addition to this," Anne raises a shot glass of clear beautiful delirium to my own glass, "he was an *opium eater*."

"I agree with Anne, but why are we talking of Branwell? It was forced work to even speak with him," says Charlotte.

The third stop on The Rum Trail is The Liar's Club, and in a drunken haze I'm wondering why I traveled all the way to England to visit a bunch of Tiki bars. But then I remember that I'm in the company of the authors of *Jane Eyre*, *Wuthering Heights*, and *The Tenant of Wildfell Hall*.

"I want to go home," says Emily.

"If you're going to pine for home, we might as well go back to speaking of Branwell," says Anne.

"My attendance at his funeral was the last time I left the house," Emily says.

"Yes, we remember," says Charlotte.

"What's the next establishment?" asks Anne.

The evening is a whirlwind and I'm shocked at how inebriated we are in what seems so short a time. Then again, we are on The Rum Trail.

"Sandinista," I answer. "It's just off St. Ann's Square."

"Of *course* it is," says Anne, before dissolving into giggles.

"I can't believe how drunk we are," I say.

THE RUM TRAIL

"Why not?" asks Anne. "If you think I've no notion of alcoholism and debauchery, you haven't read my work."

"I miss home," says Emily.

"That's where we're going right now," assures Charlotte. "Haworth has been renamed Sandinista," she lies.

"Lovely," says Emily.

Sandinista is rocking. I'm a bit worried about the Brontë sisters, but as we enter they approach the bar without hesitation, eager for the next libation. This is our last stop and I feel the need to glean whatever I can.

"What advice do you have?" I blurt out.

"Don't live next to a church graveyard," says Charlotte.

"Amen," says Anne, then looks at her older sister. "How long did you live?" she asks.

"Thirty-nine," answers Charlotte.

Anne, who lived to be 29, gasps as if this is as scandalous as embarking on The Rum Trail with the Brontë sisters.

"There's more," teases Charlotte. Anne and Emily lean in with anticipation. "I died married and pregnant," she confides.

"We'll be needing more alcohol," announces Anne to the bar at large.

"I miss home," sighs Emily.

"Do you happen to know how long our father lived?" asks Anne.

"He made it all the way to 84," I say.

"Well," says Charlotte. "Apparently consumption was reserved just for us ladies."

"Brother Branwell died of the consumption, too," points out Emily.

"Right," agrees Anne, "consumption with a dose of opium on the side."

"Tell me the situation is improved," demands Charlotte.

"In terms of TB or opium?" I ask, not sure what my answer would be in either case.

"I wish we could have opened up our school," says Emily.

"There's no use getting romantic about the past," says Anne, "so we might as well go back to that first place with the bare-chested barman. What was that place called, again?" she looks at me.

"Keko Moku," I answer.

I'm at that delicate place where you know one more drink will destroy you, but their lives seem such tragedies that destruction would be fitting. As if on cue, a waiter brings a round of Ron Zacapa Centenario. It's £8 a shot, aged 23 years and comes from Guatemala. Who am I to argue?

"On to Keko Moku," cries Anne. "And then Glass Town! Verdopolis!"

"What about the moors?" asks Emily. "I miss the moors!"

"Just shoot me in the head and call me Agnes," slurs Anne.

"Anne's right," says Charlotte, "let's go back to that first place."

"I'm really drunk," I admit. "Can you guys make it on your own from here?"

"Of course we can," says Emily.

"We'll drink your share of rum," adds Anne.

"Tell them the Bell brothers are en route," says Charlotte.

"Will do," I smile. "Will do."

EMILY DICKINSON
DWELLING IN POSSIBILITY AND PARANOIA

BY ELAINE AMBROSE

I raised the heavy knocker on the front door of the Dickinson family homestead in Amherst, Massachusetts and allowed it to fall with a thud. Emily's note said to arrive sharply at 5 pm, so there I stood with a sack from Barselotti's Bar, two bottles of wine – one white and one red – a wine opener, and two glasses. I waited a few moments and then slowly opened the door. The parlor smelled of musty leather furniture and oil lamps. Books and papers were scattered across a wooden table under a ticking clock, and a fire hissed in an old iron stove.

"Are you here?" I called.

"I'm over here, behind the door," she said softly. "Just come over here and sit down on the chair. I'd rather stay on my side."

I closed the front door and moved to a single chair facing her bedroom door. I opened the white wine and placed the bottle and a glass near the inch-wide opening. A pale, wrinkled hand reached out and snatched the bottle.

"I won't be needing the glass," she said. "I'll be with you in just a minute."

I opened the bottle of red wine and poured a large glass, wondering how to begin my interview. My drink was almost gone when I heard her set down her bottle and heave a heavy sigh.

"Thank you very kindly," she said, opening the door another inch. I couldn't see her face, but I noticed her white cotton skirt and felt the presence of a mysterious woman. "I do like my wine."

"Could you open the door just a bit more so we could talk? It's cozy out here by the fire."

"Oh, no!" she shrieked and slammed the door.

"I'm sorry," I said, gritting my teeth. "I didn't mean to offend you. It's fine if we just chat like this, you on that side, me on this one."

I gulped the rest of my wine and poured another glass. She opened the door two inches.

"I prefer extreme seclusion," she said. "In this room I wrote more than 800 poems. And I gave up my life to stay here to care for my dying mother. How in the hell did I know it would take her 30 years to die?"

I couldn't tell if she was being sarcastic, so I remained quiet as the clock ticked on the wall and the fire crackled in the stove. I heard her take another long drink.

"Thank you for agreeing to see me," I said.

"Well, you bothered me for so long that I had little choice. Excuse the condition of my house. I haven't cleaned it up in a few decades. It's a museum owned by Amherst College, but they only open a few hours during the week."

"May I call you Emily?" I asked. "That's what I named my daughter."

"That's my name. But it sounds more poetic if you use the entire name, Emily Dickinson. I do like to write in trimester rhythms."

"As in one of my favorite poems," I said.

> *"Hope is the thing with feathers*
> *That perches in the soul*
> *And sings the tune without the words*
> *And never stops at all."*

"You recite it well," she said. I heard her take a swig from the bottle so I poured myself another glass. I was relieved that she was getting friendlier by the drink.

"I'm Nobody!" she said suddenly. "Who are you? Are you Nobody, too?"

"How dreary to be Somebody!" I answered.

She laughed faintly. "One of my favorite poems," she said.

"You never lived too far from Amherst," I said. "Is that because your grandfather founded Amherst College?"

"I had no desire to be anywhere else but in my house," she answered. "All I ever needed were the hills, the sundown, and my dog Carlo. For the last 20 years of my mortal life, I preferred to be alone and I only talked to people from the other side of the door. You are most fortunate that I agreed to talk with you here today."

"Thank you," I said, as I imagined how strange we must look talking to a door. I poured another glass of wine.

"I travel within my seclusion through my library," she continued. "As I've written, there is no Frigate like a book to take us lands away."

"You must think in poetry," I said. "Did you always want to be a poet?"

"I should have been a gardener," she replied. "I studied botany and tended the gardens around my home. One summer I collected 424 flowers and pressed them into a leather-bound book. I loved the pansies, hyacinths, sweet peas and daffodils. I often sent my friends gifts of flowers with verses attached. They valued the posies more than the poetry. My poems were never famous back then."

"Didn't you instruct your sister to burn all your papers after your death in 1886?"

"Yes, I did. Lavinia burned most of my correspondence, which included hundreds of personal letters. But she didn't burn my manuscripts. There were 40 notebooks locked in a chest. My brother Austin, his wife and my sister fought over them, and finally divided the poems between them."

Just then I heard her slam down her wine bottle in disgust. "They edited my poems," she spat out the words. "They changed punctuation and reworded some lines. I loved my poem, 'I taste a liquor never brewed.' But they changed the last two lines from 'Not all the Frankfort berries yield such an alcohol!' to 'Not Frank-fort berries yield the sense such a delirious whirl!' They had no right to ruin that poem."

I poured another drink and tried to soften her irritation.

"But they did manage to publish 115 of your poems in 1890 in a volume titled *Poems,* and the book was a financial and literary success," I said. "Your books of poetry continue to sell and you are regarded as a major American poet."

I could tell she was taking a long drink. "I don't care about fame," she finally said. "Just bring me the sunset in a cup."

"I appreciate those words," I said. With the amount of wine I'd consumed, I would have appreciated an aspirin in a cup. I tried to focus again on her writing.

"Can you tell me how your family influenced your writing?"

"Well, my father, brother and sister were warm and support-ive," she said. "My mother was a cold brute. She was bedridden, and my sister and I took care of her. I did most of the cooking be-cause I love to bake. My sister and I never moved away, never got married, and never had children. My father died in 1874, and the funeral was in our home. I stayed right here in my room."

Emily became quiet, and I wondered if she was still awake. Then I heard the empty bottle hit the floor.

"They all died," she moaned. "Everyone I loved always died. Maybe you shouldn't get too friendly."

I laughed and hoped she was joking.

"I wrote the most poems between 1861 and 1865," she contin-ued. "Many of them portray my fascination with illness, dying and death. Oh, I loved to write about different methods of death. I've used crucifixion, drowning, hanging, suffocation, freezing, prema-

DWELLING IN POSSIBILITY AND PARANOIA

ture burial, shooting, stabbings and beheadings."

I finished the last of my wine and reflected on her words. I hoped she wouldn't start talking about funerals and starvation.

"Just imagine a funeral in your brain," she said. "Don't you ever want to write about thirst and starvation? That's how I feel most of the time, unless, of course, I'm writing religious gospel poems. Then I'm more intense than a country preacher. I proclaim the gospel to the entire world from my little room behind the door."

"What about love?" I asked, trying to focus on a more positive way to end the interview.

"That I shall love always, I argue thee that love is life, and life hath immortality," she said. "Till I loved I never lived."

"But you never married," I said.

"Well, I had many friends, men and women," she said. "That doesn't mean we were intimate. That means I had many friends, men and women. I wrote hundreds of letters to my dear friend, Susan, and she edited some of my poems. But she was married to my brother. I chose how my life would be, and I chose solitude."

I placed my empty bottle and glass into my sack, and stood to leave.

"Where do you live when the museum is open?" I asked, not sober enough to realize the absurdity of the question.

Without missing a beat, she answered. "I dwell in possibility."

DRINKING WITH DEAD WOMEN WRITERS

CARSON MCCULLERS
QUEEN BEE

BY AK TURNER

We're at The Duplex in Manhattan. I'm not generally a fan of piano bars, but thought it might be appropriate. We arrive early, before the real show starts. I want piano, but not so much that we can't have a conversation.

"At one time my intention was to be a concert pianist," she says.

"I know, that's why I picked this place."

She studies me with a placid face and weary eyes. "You know a lot about me?"

"A little," I nod.

"I suppose you'll want to talk about Reeves?"

"I would."

"Not until I have a drink."

As if on cue, the bartender brings us martinis. I'm not a martini drinker, but Carson has decided that I'll have one anyway. Her paralyzed left hand sits limp in her lap. She uses her right to bring the drink to her mouth. I can tell she approves. I sip mine tentatively, feeling like a child playing dress-up.

She first married Reeves when she was only 20, in 1937. They divorced in 1941, but remarried four years later. I sit patiently, letting her make her way through half the martini before I ask, "What made you get back together?"

"The tyranny of pity," she says.

"You remarried him because you felt sorry for him?"

"Well, it certainly wasn't my will to become involved again."

"I don't understand," I admit.

"No, you don't." And with that she appears to have given up on me.

Since I've fallen from her good graces, I figure I might as well go for it.

"Did you ever feel bad about leaving that day?" I ask.

"Which day? The day he wanted us to hang ourselves in the French countryside?"

"Yes, that's the day."

"You think I should have remorse over fleeing from a man who wanted me to commit suicide with him? Bartender, I'd like another martini."

"Can I get a rum and diet?" I add.

"Give that to me," she slides my martini in front of her and sets to work on it for a moment before continuing. "He'd decided to die. It wasn't my job to save him, only to make sure he didn't take me with him."

I feel my heart pounding; it's an erratic drum. I'm disappointed by this interaction. I knew she'd be weird, but I'd hoped for a kinship or friendship, and it's not there. She's not simply weird, but also disconnected, something I hadn't counted on. This leaves me melancholy and lonely. But that, I realize, is exactly what I should feel when having drinks with Carson McCullers. My rum and diet arrives and I suck it down with determination. I no longer care whether or not I have my wits about me while in her presence.

"You know, Reeves was the only man I ever kissed." Her demeanor has changed. She's wistful, nostalgic, almost as if she's sensed my disappointment and made a sudden attempt at temporary sweetness.

"I find that hard to believe," I say.

"You think I'm lying?" she challenges.

"I'm not sure. Both you and Reeves are reported to have had numerous affairs with partners of both sexes."

"Believe everything you read, do you?"

"Not necessarily," I say.

"Besides," she adds, "affairs don't necessitate kissing."

Conversation with McCullers exhausts me. I order another drink, a double this time, and decide to switch gears.

"I'm amazed that you wrote *The Heart Is a Lonely Hunter* at the age of 23," I say.

"I was 22 when I wrote it."

"Sorry."

"*I'm* amazed that it takes so many other writers so long to produce something worth reading," she counters. "Then again, when you have a physical body like mine to contend with, and you start suffering from strokes in your early twenties, you have reason not to delay. Not that I'm complaining about the length of my life. Fifty years was plenty and I did not want to continue lying in that bed at the end."

"Were you in pain much of your life?"

"Yes," she nods, "but not the type you might think."

I refuse to guess at her meaning and instead study her face. She's almost impish; severely cut bangs frame her tiny face, an exaggerated nose dwarfs an almost hidden chin.

"You know, I named my daughter after you."

"Really?" her eyes light up.

"Yes. Ivy Carson."

Her eyes sour and a frown joins them. "I'm supposed to be flattered by a middle name?"

"Yes," I assert. "After all, Carson was your middle name too... *Lula*." She smiles at this, which is a first, but the smile does little to soften her, instead she just appears odd in a different manner. I've broken through a wall, but it rebuilds itself in a heartbeat. I'm high on rum and without censor. "Do you ever regret not having children?" I ask.

"My life had more than enough struggle in it without adding a child and yet another form of loneliness."

"Why would you equate children with loneliness?" I ask.

"Because that's what love is."

"Love is children?" I ask. I'm undeniably drunk, but so is she.

"Love is loneliness. Whether it is mutual or not, it is still a singular, solitary experience. And usually unbearable."

"You are a bouquet of pure joy, aren't you?" I slur.

"What did you expect?" she asks.

"I don't know."

"I'm assuming you've read my work. You know the bones of my life."

"Yes, you're right," I agree.

"So any expectations of rainbows are..." she trails off.

"Ridiculous?" I ask.

"Yes."

This sets me giggling. The word ridiculous, the disaster of this meeting. The martini I wasn't adult enough to stomach. She smiles at me again and I tell myself it's not so bad. The sounds of the piano dance between us and we resign ourselves to drink.

MARGARET MITCHELL
CIVILITY AND CIVIL WAR

BY ELAINE AMBROSE

I wanted to meet Margaret Mitchell at her family mansion in Atlanta, Georgia so we could sit on the porch, sip mint juleps, and gently cool ourselves with fancy silk fans. However, she wanted to visit the Wild West because she never saw it while she was alive. I recommended the Silver Spur Saloon in my hometown of Wendell, Idaho, and we arranged to meet on a sunny spring afternoon before the odor of nearby dairies was gone with the wind.

We entered the rustic bar and found a booth underneath the stuffed head of a mangy moose. She scooted across layers of duct tape holding together the red Naugahyde benches. "Achy Breaky Heart" played on the jukebox back by the pool tables where some good old boys were recycling last year's tall tales.

"Well, this certainly feels like an old saloon," she said as she pecked at some dried mustard on the table. She was pretty, flirtatious, and exuded Southern charm, and the cowboys and farmers in the bar stumbled in their boots as they walked by and stared.

I ordered two cold beers from George the bartender, and he scurried over with the bottles and two mugs. "This place hasn't changed in 50 years," I said. "Some of the guys at the bar have outlines of their favorite bar stools permanently stamped upon their butts."

"I love the authenticity of your farming village," she said as she looked around the room. "Of course, the South produced statesmen and soldiers, planters, doctors, lawyers, and poets. The Yankees had the low calling jobs."

"Well, we were planters, if that's what you call it," I said. "But we grow potatoes and sugar beets in southern Idaho, not cotton and peanuts like you did in the South."

"As long as you have land," she said. "Land is the only thing in the world that amounts to anything, it's the only thing in this world that lasts, and it's the only thing worth working for, worth fighting for, worth dying for."

We were silent for a minute as we swallowed our beers, and I noticed the permanent calluses on the palms of my hands, undeniable proof that I had spent my youth hoeing beets and working in the fields on my father's farmland around Wendell. I always secretly wanted to be Katie Scarlett O'Hara, the sassy, smart, and rebellious young woman living in luxury on a vast estate in Mitchell's classic *Gone with the Wind*.

"Your story fascinates me," I said, then took a drink. "You only published one novel in your lifetime and it won the Pulitzer Prize for Fiction in 1937. That is an incredible achievement."

"But 12 years later I was hit by a drunk driver while I was walking to a movie. I was only 48 and died four days after," she said. "That miserable drunk only got four months in jail."

We finished our beers and ordered another round. I noticed that George had combed his hair, tied on a cleaner apron, and wiped the mustard off his handlebar moustache.

"We don't get purdy ladies in here in the afternoon," he said as he brought our beers. "Let me know if you need anything."

Margaret smiled and cooed with a soft Southern drawl, "Darling, the only thing I want is peace. I want to see if somewhere there isn't something left in life of charm and grace."

With that, George wandered back to his place behind the bar, trying to understand what she had said.

CIVILITY AND CIVIL WAR

"That bartender with his bushy moustache reminds me of my Granddaddy Russell Mitchell. He fought in the Confederate Army during the war," she said. "He was wounded but survived to rebuild the great city of Atlanta after that damned Sherman destroyed it. My granddaddy had 12 children and my daddy was his first born. My mother was a proud suffragist and an educated and proper woman. I modeled the independent character of Scarlett O'Hara after my mother and her mother."

"What influenced your storytelling talent?"

"My mother read to me before I could read. My older relatives told me stories about the Civil War, and I was fascinated and horrified by what they said. At an early age, I read the plays of Shakespeare, and I loved the novels of Dickens and Sir Walter Scott. They all influenced my desire to write stories, and I wrote several novelettes that were never published. I was excited to go away to college to begin my journalistic career, but tragedy struck."

I set down my mug and leaned forward, eager to hear about her tragedies.

"I fell in love with an army lieutenant named Clifford Henry in 1918, but he was killed in France during World War I. Then the next year my dear mother died in the influenza pandemic. I quit college and came back home to run the house for my father. To escape the pain of these experiences, I became an incorrigible flirt, and by 1922, I was engaged to five different men."

"You sound like Scarlett," I teased.

"Yes, but Scarlett was smarter," she answered. "Of all those wonderful men, I chose to marry a mean, drunken bootlegger named Berrien 'Red' Upshaw. I kicked him out three months after the marriage! I needed to get a job to support myself so I begged for a job as a feature writer for the *Atlantic Journal Sunday Magazine*. They didn't think women could be reporters, but I proved them wrong. In four years, I wrote 129 feature articles and 85 news stories."

"I've read that you only worked at that job a few years. Why did you quit?" I asked.

"Well, the best man at my wedding was John Marsh. He had loaned my scallywag husband money to agree to an uncontested divorce, and then we fell in love. I married John in 1925 and quit my job. We lived in a little apartment in Atlanta, and it is now the Margaret Mitchell House and Museum."

"I'm happy you got rid of the dirtbag," I said. "It seems like you survived each trial, just like your heroine, Scarlett."

"Life's under no obligation to give us what we expect," she said. "And, as I've always said, tomorrow is another day!"

My mind flashed to a tearful Scarlett sprawled on the massive stairway after Rhett Butler leaves her alone. Altanta is destroyed, her best friend is dead, her only child is dead, and the one man who can handle her is walking out into the mist. Yet, in spite of the pain, Scarlett raises her tear-stained face and declares her fearless faith in another day. Cue music, fade to black.

"Your characters live in my head," I said. "Sometimes I want to find a grand staircase just so I can fall on it and proclaim that I will survive."

She laughed and ordered a final round. George brought the drinks with a packet of beer nuts and some beef jerky on a paper plate.

"Have some appetizers, on the house!" he said.

Margaret reached out and patted George's hand. "Thank you so much, my dear," she said as she batted her eyes. George shuffled back to his beer taps and the cowboys sitting around the bar raised their bottles in silent salute.

"Some people think it's quick and easy to write novels," she said. "I started writing *Gone with the Wind* in 1927 when I was recuperating from a broken ankle. I used a Remington portable typewriter and reams of paper that I organized in envelopes after I researched historical facts. I wrote the last part first and didn't finish the first chapter until years later. The final book was finished nine years after I started."

"I've read that the book was an instant success, in spite of the fact that it was 1,000 pages," I said.

"We sold it for the huge sum of three dollars each, and sold more than one million copies in six months," she said. "I can't believe the book now has sold more than 30 million copies worldwide."

George brought the bill and waited like an eager schoolboy. We tossed two twenties on the table and Margaret gave him a wink with Southern charm. I noticed his lip quivering beneath his moustache and knew he would stretch this experience into five years of tall tales for the loyal patrons of the Silver Spur Saloon.

"Any regrets?" I asked as we walked outside.

"Well, the Junior League twice voted not to initiate me," she said. "But, frankly, my dear, I don't give a damn."

DRINKING WITH DEAD WOMEN WRITERS

DOROTHY PARKER
FUG

BY AK TURNER

We're at Grape Escape on the corner of 8th and Idaho in Boise. Dorothy Parker has come to me. We'd planned, of course, to meet at the Algonquin in New York, but my flight was canceled.

"Thanks for coming all this way," I smile as I pull out the heavy wooden chair next to her.

"Well I'm dead, you know, so it seems my schedule was wide open. Don't expect me to soften for you," she warns.

"I should hope you wouldn't!" I say.

"Good. So, how does this work then? Am I supposed to tell you about me or are you supposed to already know?"

"A little of both, I guess."

"Shush! Not another syllable until I have a drink."

"Dorothy Parker just shushed me," I mumble to myself.

"Excuse me, handsome, but I need a martini." She addresses this to Israel who walks over with menus.

"We don't have martinis, but I can still be handsome," he says. "Here's a wine list."

"Pity," she says. "About the martinis, not you."

Israel beams.

"Bring us something red," she says. "I'd like a wine that brings to mind the rustle of sheets."

I've known Israel for some time. He's a shameless flirt, but I think in Dorothy he's met his match. For the first time, he's struck silent. He walks away in search of such a wine.

"Did I scare him?" she asks me.

"Just a little," I answer, "it's good for him."

"I'd rather have a bottle in front of me than a frontal lobotomy," she says.

"Agreed."

"So, what do you know about me? Rather, what do you *think* you know? Whatever it is, it's complete rubbish."

"I know that you introduced yourself to Norman Mailer by saying, 'So, you're the man who can't spell fuck.'"

"Alright, that one is true. Honestly, did you read *The Naked and the Dead*? He changed it to fug. What on earth is a fug?"

Israel approaches tentatively. "What are you ladies talking about?" he asks, setting down two glasses.

"A worthy activity," says Parker, flashing him a set of bedroom eyes.

"You brought a live one," Israel says to me. "I brought you a dry one." With that he opens a Lyeth Cabernet and addresses Parker. "Are you a writer, too?"

She ignores his question and leans frightfully close to me. "You're a writer? Want me to shoot you in the head now, while you're still happy?"

"I'll hold off for just a bit," I say.

"Alright, but the offer stands. I'll ask you again when we're on our third bottle."

"Even in death, you're still preoccupied with suicide," I comment.

"No, not preoccupied. It's funny, really, that after all of my attempts and poems about it, I drop dead of a heart attack. What a boring last line."

"Believe me," I say, "you are anything but boring."

"Oh, but it's true. It turns out that at social gatherings, as a source of entertainment, conviviality, and good fun, I rank somewhere between a sprig of parsley and a single ice-skate."

I laugh. Israel appears to refill our glasses. They're not yet empty, but I can tell he's drawn to her. "So, what's your name?" he asks.

"Dottie," she smiles. "What's your name?"

"Israel."

"Well, Israel, why don't you go ahead and bring us another bottle. With enough wine I may forget to keep my clothes on."

He smiles at me, as if I've brought her here specifically for him. He takes his deepening blush and leaves for another bottle of Lyeth.

"I just ordered another bottle of wine and we're not even close to finishing the first. We are terrible failures. Drink up and we'll remedy this mess," she commands.

"You don't seem depressed to me," I say.

"That's because you're not very smart," she answers.

"Fug you."

"Touche!" she laughs. "Of course I was depressed, but I happen not to be right now. That's the beauty of alcohol."

"What depresses you most?" I ask.

"Tedium. Tedium is far more dangerous than shock. I see no point to words that cower in safety."

"Fug safety," I say.

"Fug safety," she agrees, raising her glass to mine. We finish the first bottle as Israel arrives to open the second.

"Let me know when you've had enough wine to forget to keep your clothes on," he says. "Maybe I can help you not find them."

"Maybe," she says. Their flirtation seems to have reached a new level. I debate excusing myself, but two women walk in and Israel is forced to attend to them. I watch Parker assess the newcomers.

She leans in close again. "If you wear a short enough skirt, the party will come to you," she says.

I blink then to realize that the second bottle is gone and we're drunk.

"Don't order a third," I command. "I can't drink anymore."

"Pussy," she chides. "But you're right. Time doth flit; oh shit."

"Israel, can we get the check?" I ask.

"Sure," he smiles at Parker. "Where are we going?"

"Back to ashes, my dear. Another time."

"Ashes?" he asks. "Where's that?"

"Here," I hand him my card to avoid explaining that Dottie's actually dead.

He runs the card and brings it back, but can't find a pen.

"It figures," says Parker. "Spend the best years of your life studying penmanship and rhetoric and syntax and Beowulf and George Eliot, and then somebody steals your pencil."

"Here's one," Israel returns with pen in hand. I give him a big tip; Parker gives him a kiss on the cheek.

We say our goodbyes on the sidewalk. "Remember," she says, "I don't care what is written about me."

"I know," I say, "as long as it isn't true."

GEORGE ELIOT
UGLY GIRLS WRITE BETTER THAN MEN

BY ELAINE AMBROSE

Mary Anne Evans, also known as George Eliot, also known as Marian Evans, also known as Mary Ann Cross, seemed to have an identity crisis that suited her just fine. Her names were more attractive than her face, and she had the dubious fortune to be educated during the mid-1800s because her father feared that her plain looks would never attract a suitor.

I met George in the historic lounge of the Napoleon Hotel Paris sitting at a table near a window with a view of the Arc de Triomphe. She cradled a large snifter of brandy and motioned for me to join her. I ordered a Brandy Alexander and sat down. I took note of her long face, sunken eyes, and receding chin and concluded that my research and her father had been correct.

"Why did you want to meet in France instead of England?" I asked.

"French brandy is so exquisite," she said. "The cognac here is superior to anything I've tasted in other parts of Europe."

My drink arrived; I took a sip and agreed.

"Also, my essay 'Woman in France: Madame De Sable' was published in the Westminster Review in 1854 when I was the magazine's assistant editor. It now is regarded as a voice for the early feminist vision. But, truthfully, I just like to drink French brandy."

"I've read that you speak many languages," I said. "Is that due to your early years in different schools?"

"Oui," she smiled. "I studied French, Spanish, Hebrew, and Latin. My favorite is Greek, and many of my novels contain references to Greek literature. And at various times, my life resembled a Greek tragedy."

George drained her brandy and summoned the maitre d' who promptly returned with two fresh glasses. She enjoyed a slow swallow and then continued.

"I had an unconventional life," she said. "I grew up during Victorian England, I used a man's name, I wrote about social injustice, and I lived for 20 years with a man who was married to another woman."

"That lifestyle was probably beyond the norm," I agreed.

"But that prude Queen Victoria loved my novels! Until then, no one knew that George Eliot was a woman."

"Why George?" I asked. "I've authored books under four different names, but they were all female."

"Well, at the time, women were writing silly books about light-hearted romance and they weren't taken seriously. I received more attention and respect with the masculine pen name. My essays, poems and novels created a public commotion because people wanted to know about the anonymous writer. I even had a male imposter step forward and claim to be me! Also, the pious patrons of the day didn't approve of my living arrangement with George Henry Lewes."

"Too bad that he was married," I mused.

"Well, his wife had at least four children by another man, so the relationship wasn't all that solid, if you know what I mean," she said. "We staged our own private wedding and honeymooned in Germany. I briefly changed my name to Marian Evans Lewes but went back to George Eliot. I love making all the rules. As I've always said, the strongest principle of growth lies in human choice."

"Tell me about your writing career," I said.

UGLY GIRLS WRITE BETTER THAN MEN

"Back in 1850 when I was 31, I moved to London and met John Chapman. He was a radical publisher and owner of *The Westminster Review.* I moved in with him, wrote essays for the *Review,* and he named me the assistant editor. With Chapman, I started a bad habit of being attracted to married men. His wife didn't approve of our relationship, so I moved on. That's when I met George Lewes. Yes, he was married, too, but like I said, his wife didn't care."

She finished another brandy and ordered a third. "I decided to go from essays and short stories to novels. My novel *Adam Bede* was incredibly popular. It was a catharsis for me because one of the main characters is modeled after my alcoholic mother. She died when I was 16, and I had to quit school and care for my father. All that angst found its way into the book. I believe that I'm proof against that word failure. I've seen behind it. The only failure man ought to fear is failure of cleaving to the purpose he sees to be best."

"Great quote," I said. "Which novel is your favorite?"

"I'd have to say *Silas Marner.* Or maybe it's *Middlemarch.* Both include social outsiders and political crisis. I really enjoy the deep psychological insight into my characters. There is so much richness to explore in ordinary country lives. And my beloved George Lewes always encouraged my writing. I dedicated my third novel to him. But, poor George was sick for two years and died in 1878. After George died, I married John Cross who was 20 years younger. For a while, I changed my name to Mary Anne Cross. But, alas, we were only married seven months before I died at age 61. That was considered old back then."

We savored the last of our brandy and paid the tab.

"The golden moments in the stream of life rush past us and we see nothing but sand; the angels come to visit us, and we only know them when they are gone. I lived life on my own terms. Because of my alternative lifestyle, the authorities wouldn't allow me to be buried in Westminster Abbey," she sniffed. "As if all those pompous poets and writers buried there were saints! That Abbey holds more scoundrels than Highgate Cemetery in London where they threw me. Highgate was the place for dissenters and agnostics."

"Any final words, George?" I asked as we prepared to leave.

"Blessed is the man who, having nothing to say, abstains from giving wordy evidence of the fact."

With that, she perched her empty snifter on the table, turned up the collar on her Victorian coat, and headed for the Champs-Elysees.

VIRGINIA WOOLF
DRINK ONLY WINE

BY AK TURNER

We're at the Cock Inn in East Sussex, and while it may not be appropriate to stuff my face in front of Virginia Woolf, I'm starving. After she places our order for a bottle of red wine, I tack on a steak and ale pie.

"Yes, lovely," she agrees. "I'll have the sausage and mash."

"Would you like to take off your coat?" I ask.

"No," she says. "I have a chill." Her hands are in her pockets and she uses them to wrap the coat tighter around herself. I notice then that her hair appears damp. It is long and flows in waves over her shoulders. I hear the sound of clinking stones. Her hidden hands are fingering the stones in those pockets and I imagine her walking not into the river, but out of it to meet me here for lunch. The wine arrives and she mercifully releases the stones and brings her hands into view.

"Thank you," she says to the barman. "And I'll not have water, only the wine."

"You'd like water, you say?" he asks.

"No," she corrects him. "I'll *not* have water. Only wine."

"Right, then," he nods, a bit confused.

"Tell me about the *Dreadnought* Hoax," I request. "I've seen pictures, you look pretty believable."

"Yes, our disguises were perfect. It was Cole's idea. There were six of us and we dressed up, convinced the Royal Navy we were Abyssinian royals, and were welcomed to the HMS *Dreadnought* with an honour guard. It was great fun, of course, though the Navy was less than pleased when they found they'd been fooled."

"Were you nervous?"

"Not at all. The worst part was that we couldn't eat or we'd ruin the makeup. We were starved by the end of it."

As if on cue, my stomach grumbles. The barman arrives in response with our comfort food.

"Was that the Bloomsbury Group?"

"In part," she said. "The Bloomsbury Group was really just a group of friends with shared interests. The *Dreadnought* Hoax brought us more into the public eye, but we weren't nearly so formal as to have membership. I'm amazed that so much has been made of it."

"Leonard was a part of it, too?"

"Yes," she confirms. "We founded Hogarth Press together, Leonard and I. I'm not quite sure why so many are up in arms about self-publishing these days. It's nothing new."

I refill our glasses. "Tell me about Leonard."

"He was a wonderful man. He brought happiness into my life. I wrote him a letter before I went to the river, letting him know that. I wanted to make sure he knew that. It was so hard for me to put words on paper then, though. I could barely think and it was all very painful." She pauses, looking down, then brings her eyes up to meet mine. "We may have to have a second bottle."

"So we shall," I agree.

"Writing was the one element of life that I retained from start to finish. Whenever I was ill or mad, writing was still there. Maybe that's how I knew it was time to go. Madness took me to the void of even writing. Did Leonard live long after I died?"

"Another 28 years," I said. "He remarried."

Her brow furrows, but only for a second. Then she smiles.

"Good."

"You had women in your life, as well?"

"Yes, of course, though our friendships were far more important and notable than the sexual relationships, though often that's what people want to remember. I loved Vita very much, but our friendship was decades long. Our sexual encounters were a very small piece of that."

"You wrote *Orlando* for her?"

"She had much to do with it, yes."

"Can I ask you why you walked into the river? I mean, not why you did it, but why you did it *that* way?"

"The river flows away from everything that is here, which is all that I couldn't bear. Which isn't to say I wouldn't do it differently if I could. I never anticipated it taking three *weeks* to find me. I'd rather be found right away or not at all, wouldn't you agree?"

"Yes, I guess so." Though I'd rather go with the flow of the wine more than the river, I think. I try not to lick my bowl, no longer hungry but still wanting something more.

"Would you like some of mine?" she asks, pushing her plate of half-eaten sausage and mash my way.

"Oh, no thank you," I answer, but still pick at her food with my fork. I feel like there would be something wrong with forgoing the opportunity to eat Virginia Woolf's leftovers.

We work our way through a second bottle of wine. I pick up the corks, wanting to take them as souvenirs.

"Not both," Virginia stops me. "You take one and I'll take one," she says. "A cork is light and my pockets are heavy. Here." She pulls a smooth stone from her pocket and places it on the bar. "Take this as a second souvenir."

"Thank you," I say. I'm about to ask her to autograph it, then realize that I'm drunk and she's dead so I probably shouldn't.

"It's time for me to go," she announces. We've spent two hours at the Cock, though her hair appears as damp, and she just as chilled, as when we first sat down. "Let's finish this wine because we can."

"Let's," I agree. We drink the last of it faster than is advisable. I put on my coat and Virginia, who never removed hers, simply draws it tighter around herself. As we walk to the door I wish for something profound, or at least memorable to say to the author of *A Room of One's Own*.

"Thanks again for the stone," is all that I can manage.

"You're welcome," she says. "Remember, it's a souvenir only. Don't let it weigh you down."

EDNA ST. VINCENT MILLAY
BURNING THE CANDLE AT BOTH ENDS

BY ELAINE AMBROSE

Edna St. Vincent Millay sat in a worn wicker chair on the porch of Steepletop, her country home in New York. As I approached, I noticed her delicate features were in stark contrast to her unruly red hair and the mischievous twinkle in her eyes. She motioned for me to sit down and poured me a glass of red wine.

"Thank you," I said as I settled into a chair on the porch. I sipped the dry wine and nodded my approval. She winked at me in return. I passed that off as nothing more than a friendly gesture.

I was eager to talk with her because I had appreciated her poetry since I first studied her work in college. Once, as a pining student, I had recited one of her poems to an absent lover:

> *Where you used to be,*
> *there is a hole in the world,*
> *which I find myself constantly*
> *walking around in the daytime,*
> *and falling in at night.*
> *I miss you like hell.*

I don't remember the lover, but I'll never forget the poem.
"You won the Pulitzer Prize for Poetry in 1923 for 'The Ballad

of the Harp-Weaver,'" I said. "What was your inspiration?"

Edna's dazzling eyes dimmed just a bit as she reflected on the power of the poem. "My mother was very poor," she said. "She left my bum of a father and took her three daughters and nothing else. We survived on the good will of friends and family. Though we lived in absolute poverty, my mother had an old collection of classic literature, and every night she read to us. My poem speaks of a poor mother's devotion to her children, giving them all that she had."

"That must have been a difficult childhood," I said.

She reached over and took my hand. I downed the glass of wine to soothe my discomfort. She smiled and released her grip.

"It's not true that life is one damn thing after another," she said. "It's one damn thing over and over."

We refilled our glasses and settled into a comfortable conversation.

"When did you begin to write poetry?" I asked.

"I started writing as a teenager because the words kept coming," she replied. "I won a poetry prize when I was 14 and was published in a children's magazine at age 15. I wrote 'Renascence' at age 20 and it made me famous. I was reciting one day at the Whitehall Inn in Camden, Maine, and a woman named Caroline B. Dow was so impressed that she offered to pay for my education at Vassar College. Of course, I took the offer."

"Your 1920 collection of poems titled *A Few Figs from Thistles* shocked many readers with its focus on female sexuality and feminism," I said.

"Well, I was openly bisexual and some of the proper people of the day couldn't relate to that," she said. "But we all had so much fun and I believe that beauty is whatever gives you joy. And what should I be but just what I am? Here's one of my favorite poems:

So up I got in anger,
And took a book I had,

BURNING THE CANDLE AT BOTH ENDS

And put a ribbon on my hair
To please a passing lad.
And, 'One thing there's no getting by –
I've been a wicked girl,' said I;
But if I can't be sorry, why,
I might as well be glad."

We finished our wine and she filled our glasses again. Then she opened another bottle, winked at me, and tossed the cork over the banister. It was becoming that kind of afternoon. I sipped the wine and waited for her to continue.

"I love humanity, but I hate people," she said. Noticing my confusion, she added, "You see, I am a poet, and not quite right in the head, darling. It's only that."

"Well, you were strong enough to be a prominent feminist during the 1920s," I said.

She laughed out loud and tossed her red hair, still determined to be the rebel flirt.

"Can you imagine?" she chuckled. "It was during Prohibition when all the rules were upside down. Really, so much good whiskey was thrown out and wasted by those prim and proper prudes. All they really needed was a tall drink and a good romp in the hay!"

"That's the answer to a lot of life's dilemmas," I said, not feeling any pain.

We started on the second bottle, and the laughter and stories continued.

"I married a man named Eugen Jan Boissevain in 1923. He took care of the house while I wrote. How wonderful is that? We bought this property in 1925 and built a barn from a Sears Robuck kit, and I had a little writing cabin and a garden. Poor Eugen died in 1949, and then the next year I fell down the stairs and died alone. I was only 58. Now this property is a museum with a Poet's Walk that leads to my grave."

"I've read that you had an open marriage," I said, feeling bold and curious.

"Well, we were married 26 years, and we both had affairs," she said. "Of course, I found that my relationships with other men and women inspired many of my sonnets. My dalliances only strengthened my art."

"Of course they did," I agreed. "Nothing kindles artistic passion more than a few decades of bisexual affairs."

"I was commissioned by the Metropolitan Opera House to write a libretto and it was well-received," she said, a bit defensive. "I also wrote a drama in verse for Vassar College about love between women. It's titled *The Lamp and the Bell.*"

She paused, smiled, and filled our glasses again.

"After I died, *The New York Times* called me an idol of the younger generation during the glorious days of Greenwich Village," she said. "Not bad for a poor girl who was named for a hospital. My uncle's life was saved at St. Vincent's Hospital in New York right before I was born, so that's how I got my middle name."

"That wouldn't have worked for me," I said. "I was born in an Army Depot and that's not an attractive middle name."

"Yes," she agreed. "It's best to have a saint attached to your name, especially if you're in need of absolution."

"You had other names, too," I said.

"Yes, I used to call myself Vincent," she replied. "And I also used the pseudonym of Nancy Boyd, and sometimes I went by E. Vincent Millay. I guess I had an identity crisis of some sort!"

"How do you want people to remember you?" I asked. By then I barely remembered my own name.

"One of my favorite poems goes like this:

> *This book when I am dead will*
> *be a little faint perfume of me.*
> *People who knew me well will say,*
> *she really used to think that way.*"

BURNING THE CANDLE AT BOTH ENDS

"My favorite poem of yours is this one," I said,

> *"My candle burns at both ends;*
> *it will not last the night;*
> *but ah, my foes, and oh, my friends –*
> *it gives a lovely light."*

"I once wrote about the sadness of growing up," she said.

> *"Was it for this I uttered prayers,*
> *and sobbed and cursed and kicked the stairs,*
> *that now, domestic as a plate,*
> *I should retire at half-past eight?"*

With that she noted the time and indicated it was time to go. She winked one last time and nodded goodbye, taking the empty bottles and glasses into the house. As I turned to go, I noticed her lighting candles. Her pensive eyes sparkled in the lovely light.

DRINKING WITH DEAD WOMEN WRITERS

FLANNERY O'CONNOR
BIRDS OF A FEATHER

BY AK TURNER

"Where are we?" she asks. Her voice is higher in pitch than I anticipated. I vow to put any further assumptions in check. She's been dead for almost half a century, so I have no right to them.

"It's called Buffington's," I answer. "I thought it was funny because their website is EatInTheBuff.com," I grin.

"Their what?"

"Never mind."

I'm sad to realize I started my one and only interaction with Flannery O'Connor with two errors. I mentioned a website, which isn't part of her vocabulary, and my humor puts me on par with that of a thirteen-year-old boy.

"I almost chose Blackbird Coffee, which is just next door, because of the whole bird thing."

"Bird thing?"

"Yeah, you know, you and birds," I mumble. We haven't even started drinking but I'm already an idiot. That's the problem with Flannery O'Connor. I like her too much, spent years carrying around her collected works like a would-be assassin with *Catcher in the Rye*.

"Never mind," she says as we shuffle in. "But I don't need to sit across from a mirror," she instructs. "I've never understood that practice. I already know what I look like."

Her aluminum crutches look cumbersome, though she's surprisingly agile. Still, I don't want to make her go far, so we sit at the end of the bar, Flannery butted up against windows to the street, which she doesn't seem to mind. She studies the cars outside and I wait for her to comment on them. Their shapes must seem foreign. Instead, she spies the bumper sticker of one parked outside. It reads: Total nonretention has kept my education from being a burden to me.

She looks at me, then back at the bumper sticker. "I said that," she states.

"I know. That's why they have it plastered on their car."

"Well, I guess people still know who I am, then."

"More than you realize."

"What'd you like?" The bartender interrupts. In a second he chalks Flannery's appearance up to that of a crazy tourist. Most of the writer types don't go so far as dressing the part, but they are equally odd in other ways.

"I'd like a Coca-Cola and coffee, please," says Flannery.

He looks at me, as if to say, "Is she serious?"

I wave aside her scowl. "Whiskey and coke, two please." He nods and leaves.

"I like *coffee* with my Coca-Cola."

"Well, we're supposed to have a drink, so like it with *whiskey*, just this once."

"I never understood why so many writers were drunks," she says. "If you want to set your mind typing, it's cortisone that will have you writing day and night."

"Really?" I'm intrigued.

"Believe me," she says somberly, "I know my cortisone."

The drinks arrive. We're thirsty and the whiskey's a slow burn with the sweet of soda. We finish them fast and in silence. I motion to the bartender for another. I want the day and the drinks and

Flannery to go on forever. Just as I'm growing concerned with her silence, she speaks, as if desperate to ask something before it's forgotten.

"My mother, did she live to be a hundred?"

"Ninety-nine."

"Figures. So that means she died in..."

"1995."

"I can count," she says.

"Sorry."

She eyes me as if sizing me up. I find myself bracing for either a violent kiss on the mouth or a slap across the face.

"You were just a baby when I died." No kiss or strike is forthcoming, she was just gauging my age.

"No, I was actually still 12 years away from being born." Now she looks as if she may, indeed, slap me.

My words are growing muddled; it's the whiskey. I wonder if it's having the same effect on her. I don't want to ask.

"You've won a lot of awards since you died, you know. People study you."

"You mean they study my writing."

"That, yes, but they also look to you and your life." We finish our drinks in sync, sucking the remnants of our cocktails noisily through tiny red straws.

"Well, the world must be terribly boring."

I'm not sure that we've asked for a third round, but the bartender brings it. His name is Sammy.

"Should I call you Flannery or Mary or Miss O'Connor or what?"

"I don't think there's much reason to worry about it at this point, do you?"

"No."

"What about Betty Hester? Is she still alive?"

"She killed herself in 1998. She was 75."

"I can count," she says again.

DRINKING WITH DEAD WOMEN WRITERS

"Sorry."

"She shot herself?" she guesses.

"Yes," I confirm.

The whiskey is seeping in fast, hyping up my mind on words. Of the situation, what's strange at the moment is that this is my first visit to Georgia. Buffington's is on Hancock Street in downtown Milledgeville. I look past Flannery to the street outside. A kid walks by in a Danzig t-shirt, which makes me think of The Misfits which leads me to *A Good Man Is Hard to Find,* the title story of one of O'Connor's short story collections. Kevin Bacon's got nothing on Flannery. It takes only three degrees for me to relate the world back to her.

We are not far from Andalusia, which sounds much grander than it is, where Flannery spent the last 13 years of her life. As if reading my mind, she tells me she'd like to visit. "For the peafowl. I want to see if I can spot any of the descendants of my flock."

"I'm sorry, but there aren't any. I mean, they have peafowl there, yes, but none with connections to the birds you knew."

We are halfway through our third round.

"I have to tell you," she looks at me intently and I'm determined to achieve sudden sobriety so that I might not miss a word of whatever wisdom she's about to impart. "At this very moment, I prefer my Coca-Cola with whiskey than with coffee. I thank you."

"You're welcome," I beam. "Is a peafowl like a peacock?"

"A peacock *is* a peafowl. Peacocks and peahens are peafowl."

"Oh," I think on this and struggle to keep the words straight in my head. "So there aren't any girl peacocks?" I ask.

"Didn't you notice the word *cock*?" she counters.

We giggle then and share an order of fried pickles. As I pay the bill, she slips a peacock feather into the pocket of my coat.

LOUISA MAY ALCOTT
LITTLE WOMEN, BIG WHISKEY

BY ELAINE AMBROSE

Louisa May Alcott stood outside the Orchard House in Concord, Massachusetts chugging from a flask of whiskey. She seemed eager to go inside her family home, the setting of her novel *Little Women*.

"Hurry," she called to me. "Let's go inside because no one is here."

I hustled to her side, noticing how much she resembled the photo I had seen in my grandmother's cameo brooch. Her brown hair piled in thick braids on top of her head, and her long black skirt rustled of stiff hoops underneath petticoats and yards of silk taffeta. She pushed open the door and maneuvered her awkward outfit into the parlor.

"Just look what they've done to my home!" she snarled. "It's a gaudy gift shop."

She picked up a Mood Pillow that sold for $12.95. The tag noted that it was a top seller and that the sausage pillow was used as an Alcott family signal to identify Louisa's many moods. When the family placed the pillow upright on the couch, the girl was happy. But if the pillow was on its side, Louisa was in one of her foul moods.

"That's preposterous," said Louisa as she picked up the pillow and threw it into a display of dolls, videos, and other official memorabilia. "I've never been in a bad mood in my life!"

She picked up two Special Edition Alcott Mugs and poured the whiskey. I took a sip and gasped as the potent alcohol warmed my throat.

"So this is where you wrote *Little Women*," I said after my eyes stopped burning.

"Yes," she answered as she waved her hand at the Wee Forest Folk Collectibles. "Of course, we didn't sell any plastic mice dressed in Civil War costumes."

We walked beyond the gift shop into the back quarter of the house. Louisa spied two chairs from the original family furnishings and we sat down with our mugs. She smiled as she recognized artwork and books from her childhood.

"I guess it's nice that they preserve all this and call it history," she said. "To me, it was just home."

"I've read that you knew Ralph Waldo Emerson and Henry David Thoreau," I said. "Tell me about them."

"Well, Emerson was in a transcendental club with my father," she answered. "He financially helped us get into a house in Concord. I took lessons from Thoreau, another family friend. Nathanial Hawthorne also was one of my teachers. I didn't think anything about it at the time, but in looking back, I was quite fortunate to have so many wonderful educators."

"That's a fact," I said. "We didn't get those kinds of teachers in Wendell, Idaho."

"I've always had unusual experiences," she continued. "Our family was quite poor when I was little. My three sisters and I amused ourselves by making up stories. At age 17, I wrote a book titled *Flower Fables* for my friend Ellen Emerson, the daughter of Ralph Waldo Emerson."

"How did the Civil War influence your life?" I asked.

"My family housed a fugitive slave back in 1847," she said. "That experience made a huge impact on my life and I became an abolitionist. I served as a nurse in the Union Hospital at George-town, and my writings during that time were published under the title *Hospital Sketches*."

We finished our whiskey and she poured more from her flask.

"I could never decide which style of writing to do," she said. "I loved to write passionate, fiery novels and sensational stories using the pen name of A. M. Barnard. Then I switched to more wholesome stories for children. I must say that I was pleased with the success of *Little Women*. It was semi-autobiographical and, of course, I was Jo. I think now they call it historical fiction."

"You never married or had children," I said.

"The problem was that I fell in love with so many pretty girls and never once had a relationship with a man," she said. "In fact, the character of Laurie in *Little Women* was modeled after my romantic friend Ladislas Wisniewski."

"That's a tough name to include in a novel," I said. "It's good that you named her Laurie."

We laughed and took another sip of whiskey. The room felt comfortable, like a favorite robe.

"I've always been adamant about women's issues," she said. "I was an advocate for women's suffrage and I was the first woman to register to vote in Concord. It was only for a school board election, but I still felt the need to vote. I wrote about women's issues of the times and associated with other strong women writers. One of my favorite quotes is, 'Let my name stand among those who are will-ing to bear ridicule and reproach for the truth's sake, and so earn some right to rejoice when the victory is won.'"

She drained her mug and took a full, final swig from the flask.

"There is one thing that really irritates me," she said. "Well, one thing besides those obnoxious toy mice in the gift shop. I never received that much acclaim when I was alive, but in 2008, John Matteson won a Pulitzer Prize for writing a biography *about* me. I think I deserve at least part of that honor!"

"You bet you do!" I said, a bit woozy from the whiskey.

We stood to leave because it was getting dark and because the booze was gone.

Louisa paused for a moment at the door.

"Far away there in the sunshine are my highest aspirations," she said. "I may not reach them, but I can look up and see their beauty, believe in them, and try to follow where they lead. These are my words of advice: Have regular hours for work and play; make each day both useful and pleasant, and prove that you understand the worth of time by employing it well. Then youth will be delightful, old age will bring few regrets, and life will become a beautiful success."

Then she loaded her arms with Authentic Alcott Mood Pillows and threw them into the display of collectible mice, knocking them all to the floor. She smiled and walked outside into the sunshine of her highest aspirations.

AYN RAND
THE PHILOSOPHY OF VODKA

BY AK TURNER

I'm at the Russian Vodka Room on 52nd Street in New York with Ayn Rand. An enormous lampshade-like hat sits on her head, casting her sunken eyes in shadow. I try not to stare at it. On the bar in front of us sit blini and caviar, pickles and black bread, and shot glasses filled with red chili-infused vodka.

"Hold on," she says. "It's exhausting being dead." With that she pulls a bottle of pills from her pocket. "Benzedrine," she explains. "For fatigue."

"Я немного говорю по русский," I offer.

She pops her pills and waves me away with her hand. "No, I don't want to speak in Russian. This is Russia enough," she motions to the Vodka Room.

I'd tried to get her to meet me in St. Petersburg, the city of her birth, but she'd insisted on New York as her true love.

"Let's toast," she raises her glass. "To man's capacity to think."

We clink, exhale sharply and throw back the vodka. She reaches for the bread, I opt for the pickles. Food is an excellent chaser.

"We'll have another round," I say to the bartendress, realizing we'll be drunk inside of ten minutes.

Ayn pulls a cigarette and lighter from inside her jacket.

"Oh, you can't smoke here," I say.

"In a bar?!" She scowls at the room. "I was right then. The only power any government has is the power to crack down on criminals. Well, when there aren't enough criminals, one makes them. One declares so many things to be a crime that it becomes impossible for men to live without breaking laws."

"Yeah," I say. "But you still can't smoke here. Tell me about how you got your start in New York."

"It was fairly difficult until Cecil B. DeMille gave me a job, but I hope you're not wanting me to praise others for my successes," she hisses.

"Of course not," I assure her, making a mental note to tread lightly. "Your successes continue even after your death. Not just your work like *Atlas Shrugged* and *The Fountainhead*, but-"

"And *We the Living*," she interrupts.

"Yes, and *We the Living*, but-"

"And *Anthem*," she adds.

"Yes, and *Anthem*, but also your philosophies. You should check out the Tea Party."

"I'll stay with vodka," she says.

We clink again and down round two. I really want to try the blini, but they're closer to her and I fear she might slap my hand if I reach for them. I opt for the black bread instead and when I close my eyes I'm back in Moscow.

"When it comes to philosophies," she advises, "you need only study the three A's. Aristotle, Aquinas-"

"And Ayn Rand?" I guess, opening my eyes to half-mast.

She smiles. "And Ayn Rand."

"Let's drink more," I suggest.

"Let's," she agrees, though this time we switch gears and opt for the pomegranate vodka. "I named Leonard Peikoff as my heir. Is he continuing my work?"

I nod. "He even started the Ayn Rand Institute after your death."

"And Nathaniel, is he still clawing at my skirts?"

"Nathaniel Branden is still around," I answer evasively. "Your split with him turned into quite the public pissing match, did it not?"

"I don't want to talk about him," she says.

"You brought him up," I counter.

We're in danger of starting our own pissing match. With a level gaze we agree to let it go and drink more. The pomegranate vodka is good, but I miss the red chili heat of the first two rounds. I'm drunk and no longer worried about getting my hand slapped, so I rearrange the plates on the bar, giving myself access to the blini and caviar.

"So, why'd you write *The Fountainhead*?" I slur.

"If you don't grasp *The Fountainhead*," she says, "you are no concern of mine."

"Sorry," I say, "but I'm not here to impress you."

"Obviously."

"Come on," I say. "Work with me here. Tell me about Objectivism."

"Alright, but let's try the Espresso Vodka next."

"Agreed, though you should know I will probably pass out on the bar."

"Yes," she agrees, "I'm sure of it."

Everything is fuzzy. My vision, my tongue, the sounds of the bar. With every atom I struggle to focus on the lecture that begins.

"Now, Objectivism. There are three axioms, existence, identity and consciousness. An axiom is a statement that identifies the base of knowledge and of any further statement pertaining to that knowledge, a statement necessarily contained in all others whether any particular speaker chooses to identify it or not. An axiom is a proposition that defeats its opponents by the fact that they have to accept it and use it in the process of any attempt to deny it."

"Uh huh," I nod.

"This is too much for you, isn't it?" she asks.

"Uh huh," I confirm. At this point, I'm unable to comprehend the instructions for a game of Duck, Duck, Goose.

"Even in death," she sighs, "I'm still the most creative thinker alive."

"Well," I add, "at least you're not full of yourself."

"Truth and ego do not equal conceit," she says.

"Ok, lady, whatever you say. By the way, your hat looks like a lampshade. I've been wanting to tell you that all evening."

"Drink this," she says, pushing a glass in front of me. "It will sober you up."

"What is it?"

"Coffee."

"You're lying," I challenge. "This is the coffee vodka."

"You got me," she says. "Drink it anyway."

I do. She tells me she's going outside to smoke. I nod and put my head on the bar, knowing that this is probably the merciful end to our date.

"I'll tell you one last thing," she says, retrieving the cigarette and lighter from her jacket, "And this will be something you can understand."

"Ok," I say. "I'm listening." I close my eyes but stay awake long enough to take in her final words.

"Whatever you do, stay loyal to the achievement of your values."

Selected Works of Dead Women Writers

LOUISA MAY ALCOTT

JANE AUSTEN

ERMA BOMBECK

THE BRONTË SISTERS

WILLA CATHER

EMILY DICKINSON

GEORGE ELIOT

EDNA ST. VINCENT MILLAY

MARGARET MEAD

MARGARET MITCHELL

CARSON MCCULLERS

FLANNERY O'CONNOR

DOROTHY PARKER

SYLVIA PLATH

AYN RAND

VIRGINIA WOOLF

Louisa May Alcott
1832 - 1888

Flower Fables (1849)
Hospital Sketches (1863)
The Rose Family: A Fairy Tale (1864)
Moods (1882)
Morning-Glories and Other Stories (1867)
The Mysterious Key and What It Opened (1867)
Little Women or Meg, Jo, Beth and Amy (1868)
Three Proverb Stories (1868)
A Strange Island (1868)
Good Wives (1869)
Perilous Play (1869)
An Old Fashioned Girl (1870)
Will's Wonder Book (1870)
Aunt Jo's Scrap-Bag (1882)
Little Men: Life at Plumfield with Jo's Boys (1871)
Work: A Story of Experience (1873)
Eight Cousins or The Aunt-Hill (1875)
Beginning Again, Being a Continuation of Work (1875)
Silver Pitchers, and Independence: A Centennial Love Story (1876)
Rose in Bloom: A Sequel to Eight Cousins (1876)
Under the Lilacs (1878)
Jack and Jill: A Village Story (1880)
The Candy Country (1885)
Jo's Boys and How They Turned Out: A Sequel to Little Men (1886)
A Garland for Girls (1888)
Comic Tragedies (1893, posthumously)
The Inheritance (1998, posthumously)

JANE AUSTEN
1775 - 1817

Sense and Sensibility (1811)
Pride and Prejudice (1813)
Mansfield Park (1814)
Plan of a Novel (1815)
Emma (1815)
Northanger Abbey (1818, posthumously)
Persuasion (1818, posthumously)

ERMA BOMBECK
1927 - 1996

At Wit's End (1967)

Just Wait Until You Have Children of Your Own (1971)

I Lost Everything in the Post-Natal Depression (1974)

The Grass Is Always Greener over the Septic Tank (1976)

If Life Is a Bowl of Cherries, What Am I Doing in the Pits? (1978)

Aunt Erma's Cope Book (1979)

Motherhood: The Second Oldest Profession (1983)

Family — The Ties that Bind ... and Gag! (1987)

*I Want to Grow Hair, I Want to Grow Up, I Want to Go to Boise:
Children Surviving Cancer* (1989)

When You Look Like Your Passport Photo, It's Time to Go Home (1991)

A Marriage Made in Heaven ... or Too Tired for an Affair (1993)

*All I Know About Animal Behavior I Learned
in Loehmann's Dressing Room* (1995)

THE BRONTË SISTERS
ANNE, EMILY AND CHARLOTTE

Charlotte Brontë 1816 - 1855
The Green Dwarf (1833)
Jane Eyre (1847)
Shirley (1849)
Villette (1853)
The Professor (1857, posthumously)

Emily Brontë 1818 - 1848
Wuthering Heights (1847)

Anne Brontë 1820 - 1849
Agnes Grey (1847)
The Tenant of Wildfell Hall (1848)

WILLA CATHER
1873 - 1947

The Troll Gardens, Short Stories (1905)
Alexander's Bridge (1912)
O Pioneers! (1913)
The Song of the Lark (1915)
My Ántonia (1918)
Youth and the Bright Medusa, Short Stories (1920)
One of Ours (1922)
A Lost Lady (1923)
The Professor's House (1925)
My Mortal Enemy (1926)
Death Comes for the Archbishop (1927)
Shadows on the Rock (1931)
Obscure Destinies (1932)
Lucy Gayheart (1935)
Sapphira and the Slave Girl (1940)
Willa Cather: On Writing (1949, posthumously)

EMILY DICKINSON
1830 - 1886

Complete Poems (1890, 1955 posthumously)

GEORGE ELIOT
1819 - 1880

Adam Bede (1859)
The Mill on the Floss (1860)
Silas Marner (1861)
Felix Holt, the Radical (1866)
The Spanish Gypsy (1868)
Agatha (1869)
Armgart (1871)
Middlemarch (1871–72)
Stradivarius (1873)
The Legend of Jubal (1874)
Arion (1874)
A Minor Prophet (1874)
Daniel Deronda (1876)
A College Breakfast Party (1879)
The Death of Moses (1879)

EDNA ST. VINCENT MILLAY
1892 - 1950

Renascence, and Other Poems (1912)

A Few Figs from Thistles: Poems and Four Sonnets (1920)

Second April (1921)

The Ballad of the Harp-Weaver (1922)

The Harp-Weaver and Other Poems (1923)

Poems (1923)

The Buck in the Snow, and Other Poems (1928)

Fatal Interview (1931)

Wine from These Grapes (1934)

Conversation at Midnight (1937)

Huntsman, What Quarry? (1939)

There Are No Islands, Any More: Lines Written in Passion and in Deep Concern for England, France, and My Own Country (1940)

Make Bright the Arrows: 1940 Notebook (1940)

The Murder of Lidice (1942)

Second April and The Buck in the Snow (1950)

Mine the Harvest (1954, posthumously)

MARGARET MEAD
1901 - 1978

Coming of Age in Samoa (1928)
The Changing Culture of an Indian Tribe (1932)
Sex and Temperament in Three Primitive Societies (1935)
And Keep Your Powder Dry: An Anthropologist Looks at America (1942)
Male and Female (1949)
New Lives for Old: Cultural Transformation in Manus, 1928-1953 (1956)
People and Places (1959)
Continuities in Cultural Evolution (1964)
Culture and Commitment (1970)
Blackberry Winter: My Earlier Years (1972)

MARGARET MITCHELL
1900 - 1949

Gone with the Wind (1936)

CARSON McCULLERS
1917 - 1967

The Heart Is a Lonely Hunter (1940)
Reflections in a Golden Eye (1941)
The Member of the Wedding (1946)
The Ballad of the Sad Café, Short Stories (1951)
Clock Without Hands (1961)
Sweet as a Pickle and Clean as a Pig (1964)
The Mortgaged Heart (1972, posthumously)
Illumination and Night Glare (1999, posthumously)

FLANNERY O'CONNOR
1925 - 1964

Wise Blood (1952)
A Good Man Is Hard to Find (1955)
The Violent Bear It Away (1960)
Everything That Rises Must Converge (1965, posthumously)
Mystery and Manners: Occasional Prose (1969, posthumously)
The Complete Stories (1971, posthumously)
The Habit of Being: Letters of Flannery O'Connor (1979, posthumously)

DOROTHY PARKER
1893 - 1967

Enough Rope (1926)
Sunset Gun (1928)
Laments of the Living (1930)
Death and Taxes (1931)
After Such Pleasures (1933)
Not So Deep as a Well (1936)

Sylvia Plath
1932 - 1963

The Bell Jar (1963)
Ariel (1965, posthumously)
Three Women: A Monologue for Three Voices (1968, posthumously)
Crossing the Water (1971, posthumously)
Winter Trees (1971, posthumously)
The Bed Book (1976, posthumously)
Johnny Panic and the Bible of Dreams (1977, posthumously)
The Collected Poems (1981, posthumously)
Selected Poems (1985, posthumously)
The It-Doesn't-Matter-Suit (1996, posthumously)
Plath: Poems (1998, posthumously)
Collected Children's Stories (2001, posthumously)

AYN RAND
1905 - 1982

We the Living (1936)
Anthem (1938)
The Fountainhead (1943)
Atlas Shrugged (1957)
For the New Intellectual (1961)
The Virtue of Selfishness (1964)
Capitalism: The Unknown Ideal (1966)
The Romantic Manifesto (1969)
The New Left: The Anti-Industrial Revolution (1971)
Introduction to Objectivist Epistemology (1979)
Philosophy: Who Needs It (1982)

VIRGINIA WOOLF
1882 - 1941

The Voyage Out (1915)

Night and Day (1919)

Monday or Tuesday (1921)

Jacob's Room (1922)

Mrs Dalloway (1925)

To the Lighthouse (1927)

Orlando (1928)

A Room of One's Own (1929)

The Waves (1931)

The Years (1937)

Between the Acts (1941)

A Haunted House and Other Short Stories (1944, posthumously)

Mrs Dalloway's Party (1973, posthumously)

The Complete Shorter Fiction (1985, posthumously)

Drinking with Dead Women Writers is the first in a series.

Look for *Drinking with Dead Drunks* in the fall of 2012.

DRINKING WITH DEAD WOMEN WRITERS

ELAINE AMBROSE
AK TURNER

Mill Park Publishing
Eagle, Idaho
www.MillParkPublishing.com

Mill Park Publishing